Self-Esteem

The Complete Guide To Changing Negative Thoughts Into Positive Thoughts And Rocketing Your Self-esteem And Confidence

(Liberating Your Inner Strength And Willpower)

Arden Castro

TABLE OF CONTENT

Introduction 1

Maintaining A Life Of Integrity 5

Altering Feelings Via Behavioral Modification 32

The Most Common Obstacles To Confidence .. 38

Both Strengths And Challenges Characterise Highly Sensitive Introverts. 49

Intuition 57

Boosting One's Self-Confidence Is Beneficial To Both One's Physical And Mental Health. 63

Principles To Consider When Establishing Your Goals 67

You Will Experience More Joy And Contentment In Your Life. 71

How To Quit Thinking In A Pessimistic Way ... 83

Accept Responsibility For The Issue 87

Maintaining Command Of The Most Vital Feelings 92

How To Improve Your Own Self-Confidence 100

People Who Are More Introverted And Their Relationships... 111

Boosting One's Self-Confidence Is Beneficial To Both One's Physical And Mental Health. 134

How To Commit To A New Year's Resolution 138

Introduction

There is a very reasonable explanation for why issues with one's self-esteem are becoming increasingly prevalent in today's society. It should come as no surprise that some people have the strong belief that they do not live up to the standards that society expects of them, given the rising rates of divorce and the increased pressure placed on them to accomplish. It is difficult to be flawless, and yet we are constantly exposed to examples of people who appear to be picture perfect on the covers of magazines and on our television screens. We are also exposed to commercials for all of the items that can assist us in living up to those norms; yet, the majority of these claims are merely hype.

How do you move past such a pessimistic outlook on life once you've recognised that there's something wrong with the way you look at yourself? That is the purpose of the experiment we are conducting. We are confident that the methods that we have developed for you to implement inside these pages of this book will assist you in moving past the stage of feeling horrible about who you are. They will also help you build up your self-confidence so that you may confront the world that you live in with optimism and a positive attitude.

The techniques described in this book have been demonstrated to be effective, and it will be useful to attempt each one in turn because each of them contributes to your levels of self-assurance, although the application of a single technique may not be sufficient on its own. Therefore, read through the entire book. After you've given the workouts we provide a go, step back and take a fresh look at who you are. You will be aware of your own worth, and you won't want the approval of others to feel satisfied with who you are. This is significant because people who have issues with their self-esteem are always looking for approval from other people. You need to quit doing that right away because even if other people validate you, it won't make much of a difference in how you feel about yourself even if you do it. At the end of the day, the only opinion that matters is the one you have to live with since it is the only one you have control over.

You will learn how to be successful and feel good about yourself by consciously deciding not to seek validation from other people, which is one of the skills that we will teach you. Instead, the exercises that are included in this experiment are ones that only require the permission of one person: yourself. Figure out how to feel good about the encounters you have with other people. Learn to take pleasure in being yourself. When you finally understand it, you will never again feel that you are lacking in some way, because that is what life is all about.

Maintaining A Life Of Integrity

There is a strong connection between one's self-esteem and their honesty. To be honest is to practise the intentional act of being truthful without embellishing the truth. Integrity can be defined as the action of living up to a promise, treating people in an equitable manner, and actively participating in moral obligations. The act of being honest in one's actions and speech ultimately results in a boost to an individual's self-esteem.

As a matter of common knowledge, decent behaviour has the potential to become quite convoluted as a result of human judgement. People are, for instance, getting ready to legitimise the behaviour they have been engaging in. In order to protect oneself or another individual, a person could add something innocuous to their statement. They won't be too concerned about it at all. They will evaluate it as typical behaviour, the same way that other individuals would.

It's not hard to argue that we ought to be truthful in all we say, do, or experience, but it's important to put our words into action. In the world of business, which of the following carefully considered choices would you recommend making: When running a business, what expenses are considered acceptable while others are not? What is the actual, quantifiable amount of time that you spend working on a customer account? In what degree would you say that you are honest about the benefits that your products or services can provide? If you were to give your chief or staff criticism, would you be able to do so in an honest way? It turns our attention to a different aspect of honesty.

When we engage in conversation with other people, we will learn that respectability can be understood in a variety of ways. What one person considers to be appropriate behaviour is subject to strong disagreement from another person. In addition to this, it gives the appearance that the cultures as a whole have significant cultural differences. The utilisation of favours is an example of a typical model. It's possible that in certain societies, this level of achievement is regarded as quite satisfying. On the other hand, in a different context, it might be considered a guaranteed return on investment.

It's possible that we were raised in an environment where the boundaries of what constitutes right and wrong weren't always clear. It's possible that children and teenagers aren't mature enough to make important choices. However, now that we are adults and have our fundamental leadership capabilities fully developed, we will soon feel the repercussions of the decisions we make and the way we conduct ourselves. Because we are now adults, we are in a much better position to evaluate whether or not our current value system is beneficial to us or whether we need to make adjustments to it.

An ideal strategy for determining one's level of self-esteem would involve determining if one's decisions or activities boost one's level of confidence, or whether one experiences even a small amount of guilt as a result of those choices or activities. In addition to this, we ought to think about if there is a justification for a certainbehaviour. We ought to be aware that the majority of the time, we have a choice in what we chose, and that the final duty is dependent on the method and selection we make. As a consequence of this, we are obligated to determine what lies within our capabilities and so on.

It could go either way. The two women have both been involved in unhealthy relationships with their husbands, both of whom have battled alcoholism for the better part of their married lives. One of the ladies has been married for over two decades, while the other has been married for somewhere around fifteen years. The two wives' respective ministers had persuaded them to maintain their marriages by leading them to believe the finest possible things about their partners. Despite the fact that they understood they might reach agreement on a variety of decisions, they felt guilty about going against what the leaders of their church had urged them to do. Important choices regarding the dissolution of the unions were taken by the two of them. Both of them are aware that in order to achieve success, they need to maintain their individuality and focus on the factors that will contribute most to their well-being.

When we live another person's attributes rather than our own, we may see how twisted our circumstances can become through the unique models presented here. These women's self-esteem began to rise almost immediately once they were capable of independent thought and made the decision to focus on facilitating choice.

It would appear that the more responsibilities you take on within an organisation, the more the environment will put your truthfulness to the test. The acts that intelligent business employees take will be ones that establish their integrity and generate the ideal connotation for their characteristics.

You are the bearers of truth, and the circumstances will reveal the fact that lies behind the actions that you have made, no matter how much you might try to convince yourself of an activity that you have undertaken. People develop their intuitive understanding of one another. An individual's trustworthiness can be vindicated through such intuition.

Training will benefit you in the event that you are required to communicate openly about the stressful parts or circumstances that are associated with your work. The question that we need to ask ourselves, then, is this: in order to persuade other people of my honesty, what actions do I need to do, and how should I conduct myself? Is there congruence between my actions and the assertions that I make?

You have nothing to worry about if you have respectability because there are no secrets. When you act with integrity, you make the appropriate choice so that you won't have to take responsibility for anything. Are we losing some of our integrity as a result of the demands that come from society?

One of the most incredible deceptions is to tell oneself, "I will just know." This is one of the tricks. Only I will be aware that I am dishonest; I will understand that I am in charge of people who put their faith in me; and I will comprehend that I do not anticipate keeping my promise. The inference is that I place a high value on the opinions of other people when determining my level of self-esteem. In terms of my sense of self-worth, I am more concerned about the decisions I make for myself than I am about those made by other people. In these contexts, I believe that only my opinion is relevant and worthy of consideration.

There must be congruence between the value you hold and the way you carry yourself. It is not as straightforward as one might believe it to be. Without respectability, caring has no purpose from an ethical standpoint.

Even when people take extra precautions, they nonetheless frequently see circumstances in which integrity is compromised. One unremarkable example of this is the social conditioning that exists within our capitalist system, which encourages us to extract as much value as we can while providing as little as is reasonably possible given the circumstances. One form of this absence of substantial quality that is becoming increasingly severe is our persistently stimulated fall into a post-authentic and post-moral world. In this world, individuals do not regard the truth but instead purposefully create uncertainty and obfuscation.

What other people do is a reflection of them; it has nothing to do with you.

When I was sixteen years old, I landed my first work as a part-time shop assistant on the tills at Somerfield (which is now known as Co-Op). I had to force myself to work through the discomfort because I needed the money. In point of fact, I lucked into getting the position when they hired me for working Saturdays; however, they misunderstood, and I subsequently informed them that I was unable to work on Saturdays. Even though I didn't have a lot of self-assurance back then, I couldn't miss out on watching football with my dad on Saturdays because it meant too much to me. As a result, I began working on Monday evenings.

At that age, I wasn't interested in any kind of self-improvement or anything like that; I basically just loved football. Although I was only passable at it, I loved following Yeovil all over the country as they competed.

At that moment, I was only thinking about my studies and attempting to blend in with the crowds by doing things like buying a stupid gold necklace, having a line shaved across one eyebrow, having odd gelled hair and even shaving my head at one point. What exactly was I contemplating?

Anyway, none of this pertains to the main purpose of the story. I used to have a job in Crewkerne, which is a small town in Somerset. If I'm being completely honest, I never really liked the town, but it does now have a gorgeous Waitrose. There were some pleasant folks in Crewkerne, but there were also some less pleasant people there.

When I became eighteen years old, I had the legal right to consent to or decline invitations to consume alcoholic beverages. When a shop clerk called it out to beg for permission from a customer, a customer might occasionally respond with "yes, please." It's hilarious... (the tone here is intended to be sarcastic).

One day, my younger friend and coworker repeated so, and I politely requested the girl who appeared to be between the ages of 17 and 20 for identification. I was greeted with the words "You fucking twat! I definitely have the appearance of an adult. You fucked up your twat!" Is this anything that reflects on me? Was I some kind of fucktard?

To be honest, I'm kind of hoping that you'll respond to that question with a no, so let's just go ahead and say that.

However, when I was younger I always had the notion that I was a terrible person. In point of fact, the girl was simply dissatisfied or upset with herself and contemplating why she felt that way. It in no way reflected how I feel about myself.

Despite this, it had a negative impact on my sense of self-worth. Because of this, it is of the utmost importance to assist as many individuals as possible in developing healthy levels of self-esteem. Hurt people tend to transfer their feelings onto those around them. People who have a healthy sense of themselves would never purposely hurt another person in such a way.

In light of what took place, there was not the slightest shred of evidence to suggest that I was a fucktwit. Nevertheless, the brain, being the brain, keeps an eye out for potential threats. It looks for problems, and if someone points one out to it, it will concentrate on that problem, allowing its emotions to guide it rather than the facts.

There's one more tale I can tell you about this.

Zack, my phoney pal, was married to his girlfriend.

Zack, you should be proud of that; it's fantastic. There's a bit of unintended rhyme going on there...

Anyway, Zack returned to his house one day to find his fiancée having a sexual encounter with another man. Zack's emotions were completely wrecked, and he started crying. After that, he was in pieces for several months. Given what had recently transpired with him, this was quite understandable. Zack need some time to recover from this, but he also held the conviction that he was to blame for what had happened. But was it Zack's decision to do that? Now, Zack may have been a poor lover or neglected her, which would be his actions (he didn't do either of those things, by the way), but the detrimental action in this situation is without a question the adultery.

How exactly was Zack able to regulate or prevent the dishonest conduct of another individual?

What the acts of others say or do has no bearing whatsoever on you; other people are solely accountable for their own aberrant behaviour. You can only do your best to help people, influence them, and try to influence them. A person can only help or improve himselfif they take responsibility for doing so. You cannot alter another person.

This is exactly what irritates me when I see someone taking someone else back after they have been cheated on; it is practically telling the other person "it's ok for you to cheat." When I see someone taking someone else back after they have been cheated on, this is what upsets me the most. What gets to me the most is the extreme lack of respect for one's own dignity that someone shows by acting in this manner.

In my own life, I really had an experience that was very similar to this one, although it did not involve being cheated on in a committed relationship. When I was in my early twenties, I was dating someone, and the relationship was going well; but, I will admit that I was playing it too cool, which was by far the biggest mistake I ever made in any of my dating endeavours. I'm not very good at texting! She went on to say that despite us kissing and going on dates, she still didn't believe that I was that into her. She also mentioned that she had met someone else and wasn't sure if she wanted me or that other guy.

My response at the time was something along the lines of "I really like you, please pick me," but not quite in those words. That shows an incredible lack of regard for me as a person. I was convincing myself that I wanted validation from someone who wasn't sure if she was completely into me, and I saw that I was doing this. That girl was lovely by the way, and a wonderful person; we weren't in a relationship and were in the early dating days, but I had messed up with my approach; there have been lessons learnt over the course of the years. It's just that she wasn't emotionally into me, which is fine, but please don't take it to mean anything about who I am as a person. At the time, I was under the impression that it was.

Transform your negative thoughts into more positive ones.

Changing your mental processes is the key to reprogramming your negative ideas so that they become good thoughts instead. The move may have been deliberate or it may have occurred by chance.

The first strategy puts you in charge of your own thinking process, putting you in a better position to achieve your objective of thinking positively. Changing the focus of your attention to something more upbeat will help you feel better in the long run. In order for intentionality to be successful, a person needs to be very explicit in replacing negative thoughts with positive ones.

In a more practical sense, this can be accomplished by making a connection between formerly terrible experiences and good aspirations. An illustration of this would be shifting the way you think about a situation from one that would make you apprehensive to one that would be an opportunity for you to grow instead. Modifying one's responses to various life events may help change unfavourable circumstances into favourable ones. Building a growth mindset can be accomplished in part through the performance of this deed. You could also make the decision to steer clear of thoughts that could lead to undesirable outcomes like depression. These kinds of emotions can lead to a negative change in neuroplasticity because they foster the creation of brain connections that are harmful. Because of this, the impacts of negative thought patterns may become even more severe as a result of the formation of a system that consists of negative feedback loops.

Adopting a mindset that is more conducive to growth can help one build a greater ability to withstand the effects of adversity. A mentality like this can result in an increase in one's level of perseverance. The process of transforming negative ideas into positive ones might be facilitated further by adopting a relaxed point of view.

Acquiring new cognitive abilities can be a helpful step in the process of reprogramming your negative beliefs into more positive ones. Having these abilities will provide you with a framework that will allow you to handle the various factors that accompany difficulties or occur as they are brought up.

Your thoughts can be reprogrammed from negative to positive if you adopt a healthy lifestyle and make it a priority. Make dietary choices that are beneficial to the functioning of the brain.

Rewiring your mental processes can also be helped along by the activity of shifting your emphasis from negative thoughts to good ones. A mental exercise that requires regular repetition in order to achieve a rewiring needs the focus of the individual's attention to be directed towards positive prospects. To put this into practise, you should consider the notion that is diametrically opposed to the negative thinking process.

By altering the circumstances in which your mind operates, you may reprogram your brain to have more optimistic thoughts. You may find that the shift helps you open your mind to fresh points of view. It is well accepted that the process of neuroplasticity, which plays a critical role in the transformation of negative thoughts into good ones, can be enhanced by travelling. During times when you feel completely overworked, giving yourself some time off can be beneficial to the rewiring process. It's possible that as a result, negative feelings, which typically accompany negative thoughts, would become less intense. Changing your mental environment to one that is more hopeful might be facilitated by surrounding yourself with others who support a positive outlook.

By ridding yourself of unfavourable feelings such as anxiety, you may rewire your brain to think more positively about things. These kinds of sensations foster the support of a system that generates negative feedback.

The process of rewiring your thinking from negative to positive might be aided by making decisions that lead you to a mentally happy place.

The process of transforming your thinking from negative to positive might be aided by reducing the amount of time you spend dwelling on unfavourable situations. Maintaining a negative state of mind through meditation might lead to the development of unfavourable attitudes such as scepticism.

You may be able to rewire your ideas away from a pessimistic perspective if you take some calculated risks in the hopes of achieving better outcomes. Your ability to bounce back from adversity may improve as a result of the experience, and this may make you less susceptible to negative thought patterns. Remorse is the fuel for the negative feedback loop that can be formed as a result of hesitating to take advantage of possibilities.

Your brain can be rewired to accept a positive thought framework if you let go of negative thought processes and let go of them completely. Master the art of keeping a cheerful outlook. You are able to reach this condition by focusing your attention on the wonderful events that are taking place. A practise like this one can be purposeful, and there is a chance that rewiring will take place over time; nevertheless, for it to have the greatest possible effect on rewiring the brain, it should be exercised on a consistent basis. Experiment with several methods of thinking to identify which conceptual framework aligns most closely with your core ideals.

You may lay the groundwork for rewiring your brain to think in a more optimistic manner by practising self-acceptance and teaching yourself to have faith in your talents. A mindset like this should not be mistaken with one that engages in self-deception. Self-acceptance can be a powerful driver of success, which in turn can help to create a positive feedback loop consisting of positive mental processes.

Taking things easy is another strategy that might help you rewire your ideas and achieve a more happy mental state. You can accomplish this by bringing your thoughts to a state of peace by taking few deep breaths. While you are doing this, make it your goal to clear your mind of unproductive habits of thought. To be successful, you should make an effort to connect with your senses, for as by concentrating on the sensation of air being drawn into your chest. Shifting your focus from unfavourable feelings to the sensations in your body can help you reduce the impact of negative thought patterns. You now have the means to begin fresh with feelings that are untainted thanks to the foundation provided by this framework.

Consider the possibility that you can teach your brain to establish a foundation for more optimistic mental processes. Your efforts to alter the way you now think will be fruitless if you let doubt get in the way. You can accomplish this by viewing perceived failures as opportunities to learn something new. After you have recognised the teaching, you should concentrate on it. In everyday life, you can put this into practise by setting a goal to, for instance, keep an eye out for three positive occurrences for every failure. When extrapolated to a daily routine, this practise has the potential to rewire your brain to put you in a more happy mental state. The process of rewiring your mindset can be accomplished in essence by creating an emotion of optimistic anticipation by reflecting on the underlying causes of the wonderful events that have occurred.

Keeping your attention on happy events can make you feel motivated, which is an important first step towards developing a more optimistic perspective on life. A perspective like this can assist you in recognising the plethora of opportunities that are present in the world.

Rewiring your brain may need you to first become more conscious of the patterns of thinking that run through your head. In addition to mindfulness, concentrate on the flow of your ideas. Put your attention on happy ideas by drawing on the strength of self-awareness. With the help of this instrument, you will be able to exert control over your subconscious, which is likely the source of a pessimistic frame of mind.

You can better embrace the process of rewiring your mental state if you are aware of the effects that negative thinking has on your mental state. One of the effects is that it will make it more difficult for you to succeed. Indecision is another potential outcome of having negative ideas.

Altering Feelings Via Behavioral Modification

Keep in mind how your thoughts influence your feelings, which in turn influence your behaviour. In this stage of the process, you will be concentrating on how to modify your feelings by altering the behaviours you engage in. Overcoming behaviours can be challenging, particularly if you have developed a habit of engaging in them, but it is not impossible to do so. If you dedicate a little bit of your time to doing so, you will be able to learn how to control your behaviours in order to better manage your emotions.

Have you ever heard of the jail experiment that was conducted at Stanford? The experiment was carried out with participation from two different groups of undergraduate students who had been chosen at random. Others were selected to serve as the prison's guards, while others were selected to serve as inmates. They were all locked up in the basement of a building that had been transformed into a mock prison, and their natural behaviour was observed while they were kept there. The experiment was designed to investigate what would happen when some people were given the false impression of authority, while others were told that they had none. Participation was totally up to the individual, and it was not required of anyone. They were free to depart whenever they chose to do so. They were able to stop if that was something they desired to do.

It is essential to keep in mind that none of these inmates or guards had ever committed a crime, and none of them had ever been qualified for a position as a prison guard because they had ever been incarcerated. The incarceration process did not result in any significant loss of authority or rights. Within a matter of days, despite the fact that there was no real power holding anyone there, the prison guards began acting aggressively and humiliating some of the prisoners simply because they could. On the other hand, the prisoners were becoming depressed and were quite passive, obeying whatever they were told despite the fact that there was nothing holding them there. They did not depart despite the fact that they were free to do so. Even though just a few days earlier, they had been peers, the only thing that had changed was that they were placed in the same room together on different sides of the bars while some scientists told one group they were prisoners and the other group that they were guards. The guards became increasingly cruel as they enjoyed their perceived authority, which allowed them to demean their prisoners. This was despite the fact that the only thing that had changed was that they had been placed in the room together on different sides of the bars. The experiment was never completed since it had to be stopped prematurely due to how intense it was becoming. Their surroundings were quite literally affecting the feelings that they had.

A toxic atmosphere can cause a person to have unpleasant thoughts and feelings, which can lead to depression. On the other hand, being in a joyful and calm state might result from being in a favourable atmosphere. Altering either your environment or your behaviours can have a direct impact on the feelings you experience. You are able to deceive yourself into experiencing a variety of emotions. You are able to alter your emotional state by intentionally putting yourself in a more peaceful state. You are able to agitate yourself by engaging in a variety of behaviours. In the end, the emotional state that will follow is highly symptomatic of the behaviours that you are currently displaying.

The James-Lange hypothesis is a specific theory of emotions that postulates that one's feelings are the culmination of a series of preceding events. First, there needs to be a stimulus, then there needs to be a physical response, followed by an interpretation in the mind, and finally, all of these components need to come together to form the feeling. Therefore, if you apply this idea to emotions, you should be able to understand how you can exert control over your own feelings. Regardless of the stimuli that you are presented with, if you wish to act in a relaxed manner, taking slow, deep breaths can help you achieve this goal.

You can trick your mind into thinking that you are relaxed if you physically go through the motions of being calm. If you physically go through the acts of being calm, you can mislead your mind into thinking that you are relaxed.

People who are going through anxiety attacks are given medication to take if necessary, but they are also given tools and tasks, such as taking deep breaths, reminding themselves that they are okay, and relaxing their bodies, to stop the feelings of anxiety that were previously overwhelming them. You can see the effects of this frequently with the treatment of anxiety. People who are going through anxiety attacks are given medication to take if necessary. The methods in which we behave can have a significant amount of power.

The Most Common Obstacles To Confidence

Despite the fact that the obstacles to confidence faced by each individual are unique to their own lives, experiences, and points of view, there are some obstacles that are universal and affect everyone. The following are the top five of them:

Fear

Fear is the most typical obstacle that keeps people from maintaining their self-confidence over time. It's possible that you have a fear of failing, a fear of being rejected, or even a fear of succeeding in what you do. You can be afraid of success because it raises the bar so high and because it comes with a large number of obligations and responsibilities. On the other hand, the vast majority of your concerns are groundless. Your mind is the only area where these anxieties can manifest themselves. Take a moment to reflect on the concerns you have that make you feel less confident in yourself. Are they authentically based on any reality at all? Exists any evidence to suggest that they will become a reality? Are you worried about something that hasn't even happened yet or something that's highly unlikely to occur? Also, even if some aspect of your fear comes true, it will probably not be nearly as terrifying or limiting as you anticipate it will be.

Worry and excessive overthinking

Worry and unproductive thought loops are two more things that might undermine confidence. You may have a persistent belief that you need to appear perfect, that you are concerned with what other people think of you, or that you are afraid of making a mistake or failing at something. Worrying can become a vicious cycle, with negative thought patterns being reinforced through thoughtless repetition. It is difficult to let go of a notion after your brain has attached itself to it, much like a gerbil on a wheel.

Because you have a mindset that is far too focused on perceptions and superficial outcomes rather than on being who you are, living in the present now, and loving yourself, worry and excessive thinking are likely to emerge in you. You don't have time for anxiety when you're actively involved in something, whether it's work or play, especially if it's something that's geared towards assisting or serving other people. Your mind is preoccupied with matters that are much more significant. When you find yourself back in the loop of worrying when you have some free time, simply utter the word "stop" aloud to bring an end to the anxious thoughts that are running through your head. The next step is to refocus your thoughts on something constructive or to occupy your mind by reading, writing, assisting someone else, or producing something.

The sin of procrastination

The habit of putting things off, often known as procrastination, can rob you of your self-assurance since it subtly holds you back and prevents you from realising your full potential. If you wait until the last minute to get anything done or put something off until the last minute, your performance will never be as good as it could have been. The end result will never be as productive or confident as we had hoped. When you put off starting a task, you give yourself the impression that you are unable to do it, but in reality, all you need to do is get started. The most difficult aspect is getting up the courage to initiate the beginning of something simple.

Find out what your top priorities are, leave yourself plenty of time to do everything, and organise your activities in accordance with those goals. If you notice that you are consistently moving a responsibility to the bottom of the list, make it a priority to move that responsibility to the top of the list and complete it as soon as possible. If you keep putting it off, it will just continue to deplete the emotional energy you have available to you. Simply get started, even if it's with a single, little step; this will carry you through the remainder of the process, strengthening your confidence that you can act in similar situations in the future.

a lack of determination

It is crucial to one's ability to gain confidence to be able to make decisions, even when they are not one hundred percent certain. The presence of doubt can cause one to become immobilised, as well as inefficient and insecure. You have the ability to change by setting time limits for yourself to come to a decision and then committing to that decision. Because making a decision almost never comes with a guarantee, you should expect to experience some level of anxiety regardless of the path you pick. Getting used to the unease that comes with not knowing what will happen next is the problem. The majority of decisions are not irreversible. You are free to make a different decision if you become aware of new information that suggests doing so.

You won't be able to move forward at all if you wait to make a decision until everything is ideal. Because the perfect time will never occur, you should choose a time that is reasonable and stick to it. Making a choice, even if it turns out to be the incorrect one, is better for your self-confidence than remaining indecisive throughout the process. (At a later point in the book, I'll go into greater detail regarding making decisions.)

A question mark

It's not uncommon for doubt to be the covert agent behind all four of these other hurdles. Your lack of confidence in your abilities, intelligence, and judgement is the root cause of your anxiety, worrisome thoughts, and inability to make decisions. But if you don't believe in yourself, how can you expect anyone else to trust you?

If you have a history of making terrible judgements or using bad judgement, then you should analyse what you learned from these circumstances and how you can modify them going forward. If you have a history of making poor decisions or using bad judgement, then you should examine what you learned. This is not the case the vast majority of the time. Because we are now grownups, we have accumulated a wealth of experience, which provides us with wisdom and judgement. Simply put, we don't have faith in ourselves.

Who other than you knows what is best for you than you do yourself? You should start thinking of oneself as someone who is self-aware and possesses inner wisdom. Even if you don't trust the answers you find within yourself, they are there waiting for you to discover them. You can overcome self-doubt by engaging in a series of seemingly insignificant acts of self-trust. Find a circumstance in which you are able to function normally but in which you are experiencing self-doubt. Then you should move forward using your best judgement in spite of your uncertainties. Get in the habit of acting even when you are unsure what to do. You'll get a good workout for your self-assurance muscle.

These frequent confidence hurdles affect people of all ages and backgrounds. Fear, worry, procrastination, indecision, and doubt are all emotions that are common to all of us from time to time. However, when these feelings become so overwhelming that they prevent us from achieving success, enjoying relationships, speaking our minds, or making a living, then it is time to face them and destroy them.

Both Strengths And Challenges Characterise Highly Sensitive Introverts.

Empaths possess a great lot of strengths that enable them to live full and lovely lives and provide support for them in doing so. It will be much simpler for you to bring your empathic ability into alignment with the rest of your life once you have begun to accept your identity as an empath and have incorporated self-protection and self-care practises into your daily routine. This indicates that you can start taking use of the various advantages and benefits that come with being an empath.

When you awaken to your empathic skills and start to take control over them, you may look forward to growing and embodying many great qualities. Here are some of the strengths that you can look forward to developing and embodying:

A Major World Power

The power of empaths should not be underestimated. This is one of the many reasons why people in society look down on them so much. They are terrified of the power that they hold. You are clearly not like the normal person because you have the ability to pick up on things about other people that they might not be willing to talk about or because you have the ability to form profound connections with the plants and animals in your environment. In today's modern civilization, there are a significant number of people who live their lives in complete isolation from the rest of the world. They have difficulty tuning in on even the most fundamental levels, much less going as in-depth as you do. It's possible that you view it as a weakness, but that's only because you've been socialised to think that way. In point of fact, you hold a significant amount of authority. You will be unstoppable in your efforts to bring about positive change in the world once you have learned to accept it and work to your advantage by utilising it.

An Incredible Acquaintance

Anyone who counts an Empath among their circle of friends ought to feel an overwhelming sense of gratitude. People that are empathic are wonderful companions. Those who are empathic have a profound love for the people in their lives that they care about and will go to any length to support and safeguard them. They are able to provide excellent counsel to their buddies. When a friend is dealing with a challenge of some kind, empaths are pleased to put their wonderful gift of empathy to work by imagining what it would be like to be in their friend's position in order to gain a better understanding of the circumstance and to determine what the most appropriate course of action would be.

Capability of Identifying Warning Signs

You have an incredible capacity to recognise warning signs in any individual or circumstance, thanks to your unique perspective that allows you to see what's going on beneath the surface of things. You can accomplish this by empathising with the other person, which effectively enables you to put yourself in their position. This indicates that you are able to recognise the consistency that exists between the individual's words, actions, and feelings. There, you will be able to ascertain whether or not they are acting in a manner that is congruent with the truth, whether or not they are lying, or whether or not they are dishonest in any way. You are able to determine whether or not there is a covert agenda at play when you recognise any symptoms of incongruence.

It is an entirely separate matter whether or not you choose to really recognise and act on these, but the fact that you are able to detect them and become aware of them is a very powerful talent on its own. If you are tuned in and able to act on the information that you receive, it will be easy for you to avoid danger and energetic attacks. Because you are able to know whenever there is something inherently incorrect with a situation, it will be easy for you to avoid both danger and energetic attacks. If you are not yet, there is no need for alarm. Because you are an empath, you have the power to access this skill whenever you want. You still have time to make a change.

Finding People Who Lie All the Time

You have the capacity to swiftly identify those who are habitually dishonest, which is yet another advantageous skill you possess as a result of your keen insight into the inner workings of other people. You can tell almost immediately when other individuals are lying to you. You can identify the harmony between the person's words, actions, and feelings in the same way as you can notice the red flags. If you are able to identify any indicators of disharmony, it will be much simpler for you to suspect that someone is lying. This typically manifests itself as little more than a "knowingness" within. This provides you with the motivation to avoid from believing them and can assist you in preventing yourself from becoming sucked into and caught up in the web of falsehoods that they have spun. The more you put effort into developing this skill, the more effectively you will be able to use your talent.

If you are a wounded healer who is unable to make effective use of your gift, you may discover that you are drawn into another person's web of falsehoods. In the process of mending this archetype, if you have it, this is something that needs to be addressed, as it is important.

Powerful abilities in the creative arts

People that have a natural talent for something It is common knowledge that empaths are blessed with exceptional creative abilities. They are very skilled artists, singers, poets, writers, and creators in general, as was previously said in this conversation. Empaths have a poetic way of perceiving the world, which enables them to produce one-of-a-kind works of art that showcase their individual perspective on the world. Their capacity to imagine something in their thoughts and bring it into the material world with their imagination is simply astonishing. The majority of empaths will struggle the hardest when it comes to releasing all of the negative energy that they have taken in over their lives. This pessimism can manifest itself in uncertainties such as doubt, insecurity, fear of failing, and a general lack of confidence.

Although there are a variety of ways in which empaths might express or make use of their creative potential, virtually all empaths have the ability to be creative. To put it another way, not every empath will be exceptionally talented in the same areas, but they will all have some degree of creative potential that they may tap into to express who they are and how they want to contribute to the world. This provides the Empath with a sense of immense fulfilment and satisfaction.

Excellent at finding solutions to problems.

When an empath has developed their innate ability to feel what others are experiencing, they are in a position to be exceptional problem solvers. Because of their capacity for empathy, they are in a position to examine the desires and requirements of many parties from a variety of perspectives. Because empaths are able to examine a given circumstance and see it from a variety of perspectives, they have a significant advantage when it comes to finding a solution that will be helpful to all sides of a conflict and will be a win-win for everyone involved.

Intuition

Intuition is an abstract term, as was discussed in chapter 2, which you can read here. There is no way to learn about it other than to describe it in the same way that you encounter it, presuming that you comprehend its core concept. Your ability to process your emotions, thoughts, and experiences, as well as the sensations in your body, is made possible by the fact that it is a blend of your spiritual, physical, and cognitive aspects. It advises you on what is appropriate for you, taking into account the things that are important to you. It instructs you on how to behave appropriately in public settings.

Because it is a direct experience of the truth or a reality, intuition is unaffected by any kind of reasoning process that might be going on in the brain. Consider it to be an immediate understanding of something that you are observing or experiencing at this very moment. It is a profoundly human sensation that defies all attempts at explanation. It is a blend of both emotion and reasoning that leads you to arrive at a sound judgement based on the facts that have been provided to you.

When you confront a friend about something, that tiny voice in your head will tell you if they are not giving you the truth about something. This is something that we have discussed in the past. It is your physical self that reacts before your mental self can tell you what you wish to accomplish. Give thanks to your body for the intuitive processes that, for example, kept you safe when you were in danger. While your mind stores the ideas that you have acquired, your body provides you with actual sense data that you can trust more than your thoughts in some circumstances. While your mind stores the ideas that you have learnt, your body gives you actual sense data.

We learn from the discussion of lucid dreaming in chapter 2 that if a person can figure out how to be aware that they are dreaming, then they have the ability to exert control over their own dreams. It indicates that even while you are asleep, there is a method to differentiate between the dream and reality. Despite the fact that the vast majority of people do not possess this ability, and that is perfectly acceptable. However, this merely demonstrates that if you are able to dream of improbable events while you are asleep, you are capable of thinking creatively about challenging problems in your waking life. On the other hand, the body does not "think," as it only reacts to its environment.

When it comes to the body, you have no say in what takes place. The truth can be deduced in this manner. Because it can only react to the information that is being offered, this is how you can tell that the body language is not lying to you. The cognitive filtering process does not exist. Because of this, there is a great deal that can be gleaned by studying non-verbal communication alone, including the signals that can be conveyed through body language as well as gestures, particularly involuntary ones. We have proven that the body does not lie; nevertheless, if you plan to lie with your body language or if you are a very talented actor or actress who is doing it on purpose, you can get away with lying with your body.

Even though acting only on the basis of this intuition may not always be practical or advantageous given the circumstances, you can try to check if what your intuition tells you about a person, such as a colleague, is valid when it tells you something about that person. For example, when your intuition tells you something about a colleague. For example, your instincts tell you that this coworker is not working on the assignment that has been allocated to them, but rather of confronting them about it, you think about how you should approach them in the appropriate manner. Many people go through life ignoring their intuition for a variety of reasons. This is something that happens to a lot of people. Growing up in a family that does not encourage the expressing of feelings, whether done in an appropriate manner or not, is one of the reasons. Many young individuals, especially those who were raised in homes where discipline was strictly enforced, develop the belief that showing their feelings makes them appear to be emotionally fragile. They learn to repress their emotions instead of expressing them because they are afraid of being rejected or criticised. As a consequence of this, kids do not develop their intuitive abilities or their sense of self-confidence as they grow up. Building one's self-assurance and belief in one's intuitive abilities can be facilitated by cultivating an atmosphere that encourages the use of healthy methods for expressing one's feelings; this is one way to address this issue.

Boosting One's Self-Confidence Is Beneficial To Both One's Physical And Mental Health.

The professionals who work at the National Mental Health Centre believe that having a healthy self-esteem and sufficient self-confidence are the primary indicators of excellent mental wellbeing. As we have previously discovered in an earlier section of this book, the formation of a person's sense of self-worth typically takes place in the formative years of childhood, when the individual's parents are largely responsible for shaping both their self-assurance and their personality. Children who were raised in households that were more upbeat and encouraging tend to carry more confidence with them throughout their lives. This gives them an advantage in a variety of spheres, including academics, athletics, social skills, and even just taking better care of themselves in general. When youngsters reach their teenage years, those who have developed a healthy sense of self-confidence are more equipped to deal with the influence of their peers and are able to make choices that are in their own long-term interests.

According to the mind-body connection theory, a person's mental health can have an impact on their physical health, and similarly, a person's physical health can have an impact on their mental health. People who struggle with mental illnesses such as depression and anxiety frequently experience deterioration in their physical health, manifesting itself in symptoms such as persistent pain or a lowered resistance to illness. It is possible for a person to enhance their physical health by taking care of oneself physically, such as by engaging in physical activity and maintaining a nutritious diet. However, maintaining a healthy mental state can also assist a person avoid developing physical issues.

Because they are able to participate in a wider variety of activities, people who enjoy better physical health typically report higher levels of happiness and life satisfaction. They often have more energy and motivation to get themselves out into the world in order to accomplish things, or even just to connect with other people. People have a natural tendency to derive pleasure from the good fortune of others; hence, when they surround themselves with people who exude self-assurance and contentment, they may also start to experience these emotions themselves. People who are confident tend to hang out in the same social circles for this reason, which is why you frequently see them doing so. People who have strong mental health are drawn to others who have the same qualities and would much rather spend their time with such people than with those who do not display the same characteristics.

Principles To Consider When Establishing Your Goals

The following twenty "simple, but key principle" will jump-start your life again; they will give you new energy, excitement, and passion, and they will leap you forward from where you are now to where it is that you want to go, far more quickly than you ever dared to dream.

1. An Insatiable Craving

Having an intense desire is the first step in the process of setting goals for oneself. You can't teach yourself to have this quality; you either were born with it or you didn't. There's no middle ground. You might be able to remain focused on your task or goal for a short period of time, but if you do not have a strong desire to succeed, you will inevitably fail as a member of the team.

2 - Have One Major Goal The majority of Americans, almost 95 percent, do not have a goal. Many of the remaining 5% of Americans who do have goals have set themselves unrealistically high standards for themselves. Why does this seem to be a problem? Because you do not have any clarity if you do not have one major definite purpose or goal; you are no closer to accomplishing any of your goals than the 95% of Americans who do not set any goals for themselves at all. Your objectives ought to be very specific and easy to understand.

3 How To Achieve Your Objectives While Challenging Yourself When we are trying to achieve something, the majority of the time we do one of two things: we either set our goal too high or we set our goal too low; very rarely do we set them just right. This component of goal setting can be very challenging, particularly for

those who do not have a lot of experience working with this method.

Setting our sights too low will prevent us from realizing our full potential in terms of what we are capable of achieving and will prevent us from living a life that is self-fulfilling. We run the risk of becoming disheartened if we set our goals too high because they are so much beyond our ability to achieve them.

4 - Make Sure Your Goals Can Be Measured You should make sure that your goals can be measured only for the benefit of being able to monitor your progress. It is the same as keeping track of your progress while you are driving to your place of employment. When you drive your car to work, you are aware of the distance you have traveled as well as the distance you still need to travel.

To merely declare one's intention to improve one's physical fitness is simply not enough. How will you determine if you are at an appropriate level of physical fitness? Try instead to be more detailed; a sentence like "I run a 7-minute mile" is an example of this type of sentence. It's easy to understand, pinpoint, and quantify.

5. Put It in Writing Your Objective When you write down your objective, make sure that it is specific, affirmative, and written in the present tense. The phrase "I earn $100,000 per year" is an illustration of this. Simply putting down on paper what you want to achieve can bring it to life and bring it closer to being a reality for you.

You Will Experience More Joy And Contentment In Your Life.

I decided to start monitoring every aspect of my life rather than conforming to the consensus of society over what constitutes right behavior or going along with the flow of the mob. Because of my experiences and the way the world actually is, I was able to gain awareness when I started to focus more on my own decisions and less on what other people were saying and doing in public spaces.

a number of distinct beginning points for continuing on with a conscious life.

Ask yourself what it is that you require. How often do you fail to maintain your composure? NOT have a preference in this matter? Do you not have the remotest idea of where you should go to get something to eat? Are you unsure about what you require from the menu? Do you not hold any opinions? You are in need of a legislator or arrangement to speak for you, but you are unsure which it is? How about you ask yourself what it is that you truly require? Where do you call home now? What is it that you're craving right now? It is not improper to think one's own thoughts or hold certain preferences. You won't receive any criticism for doing so.

Do the things that make you happy. Why not spend your time on earth doing things that make you happy rather than committing a significant portion of it to fulfilling your obligations and satisfying your desires? Do not bother going to a certain get-together of friends if you detest spending time with them. If coming to your monthly get-together with your coworkers wears you out to the point of collapse, you should stop going. Find a different way to exercise that you enjoy doing instead of going to the gym if you don't like going there. Make a greater effort to participate in activities that you enjoy doing on a regular basis.

Live your life in accordance with the facts of the situation. In most cases, our thoughts and the way we conduct our lives are molded by both society and our families. What are your thoughts? Who are you, exactly? In what do you put your faith? What have you learned to be true in your life as a result of the experiences you've had? To truly live your reality, you must be honest with yourself and choose to focus on the things that have an effect on you. In addition to this, it entails being truthful with other people, communicating everything that should be expressed, and being true to your identity. Not concealing one's identity by wearing a mask.

Recognize your own unique identity. It's possible that you have certain flaws and deficiencies. It's possible that you don't give yourself enough credit for being as brilliant or capable as your colleague or your sister. The vast majority of these lies are the product of having spent a lifetime being taught that you are not good enough or that you lack something. You have not been broken. In point of fact, despite the flaws or shortcomings that others may observe in you, you are adequate. despite the fact that you may have been persuaded differently by other people. It is not necessary for you to be thinner, taller, smarter, or more prepared in order to prepare better food or earn more money. People in your immediate environment will constantly compare you to others in an effort to make you feel worse about yourself and their own place in the world. Make every effort not to be fooled by that. You will attempt to feel better by judging the actions of other people. It is important to remember not to let your sense of superiority affect how you acknowledge others.

Carry out job that is in alignment with your being. If you are engaged in work that does not stimulate you intellectually or emotionally, you should look for ways to escape it. You are free to pursue an other line of work. This is a complete post that explains the most effective technique to carry it out. If the work that you perform does not reflect who you are, then you are not yet prepared to make the most significant contribution that you can to the world. Make baby steps toward escaping your day job and engaging in employment that conveys an impression of who you are while you're at it. You can focus on your future profession or company venture in the evenings and on the weekends, in addition to the time you have after work.

Ignore the guidance and demands that society has for you. You are going to be presented with a great deal of advice and direction from members of the community, and it will demonstrate to you what you need to do in order to be happy. Find a new field of employment, get a house, get a spouse, have a child, and so on are all things that should be done. Create a savings plan for your retirement, put money into real estate, and continue your education. The way of society is just one method; it is not the only way. You have the ability to design your life so that it allows you to focus on the things that are most important to you.

Spend your money wisely. Take care not to fritter away your hard-earned money. Make an effort not to fritter it away on meaningless things or spend it without much consideration. Do you in fact require whatever it is that you want to get in the near future? Is it a conscientious buy that will truly enhance an enormous worth in your life, or will it be a piece of rubbish that you're gathering from a carport deal? Ask yourself, "Am I in a position where I can continue my life without making this purchase? Is this purchase really so significant?" Be conscious of how you invest something that is undeniably valuable to you: the time that you have. Ask the same kinds of questions about the time that you inquired about the money. Stop wasting your time on activities that are mindless and unsatisfying and start doing something more productive instead.

Have courage as you travel. Although we can't eliminate fear entirely, we can learn to live our lives with more bravery and find ways to face challenges head-on. Fear should first be recognized for what it is, and then it should be questioned. Is there a basis for the concern? Is there a good chance that the worst-case scenario will play out? What are the possible outcomes, and how likely are they? When you are aware of your fear, you are able to go about your life being cognizant of it while at the same time giving it a secondary thought. When fear begins to subside, it's the perfect time to put some boldness into practice.

Repeat "no" one more time. Living a conscious life helps you to go in the direction of a genuine existence that you feel compelled to live and places the weight of decision-making squarely in your hands. Saying "no" more often is the most effective tool you have for maintaining a thoughtful lifestyle in the long run. Saying more "NOs" in response to fewer requests for something indicates that you do not want more. Say "no" if there is a certain food or event that you would rather avoid, such as eating it or attending it. You won't be able to say "no" to the things that really matter unless you keep building up your "no" muscle. until such time as you are able to say "no" to that management, that relationship, and that horrible way of life.

Prepare to Make an Impression!

I continued walking into the bar while dressed in my black jacket and jogging bottoms. I started to feel awkward, self-conscious, and not quite in control of myself, in addition to being somewhat out of place.

I was wearing a tracksuit bottom, an orange Adidas polo shirt, and a gold chain as I stepped into my theater lesson. (Jonny, who is only sixteen years old, bless your heart.) I had the impression that I was the only person in the room who was not like everyone else, that I was completely out of place, and that I did not even want to talk.

I went to work wearing my business attire, which consisted of a white shirt, black pants, and black shoes. I wasn't in a particularly high position in the organization, but I was satisfied with who I was. During my lunch break, I went out for a walk and felt quite at ease going into stores and walking around town to look around.

As I walked into the bar, I was sporting an Abercombie shirt, a pair of brand new pants, and some decent shoes. I experienced a sense of greatness and the confidence to approach others and converse with them.

Do the examples that have been given above imply that if you spend a lot of money on nice clothes, you would immediately feel more confident in your daily life? In no uncertain terms. What I'm trying to say is that the clothes you wear have the potential to have an effect on how you feel about yourself.

Actually, I just made the decision to include this because it was covered in one of the personal development classes I've been taking recently. This was a piece about how what you wear can not only have an effect on the initial image that people get of you, but it can also make you feel amazing, and I could definitely connect to it.

It is not solely for the purpose of impressing other people, as that would constitute seeking external validation for the experience of feeling good. Being content with who you are is of the utmost importance. Think about it: when you finally get your hands on that brand-new top that you've been coveting, how amazing do you feel when you put it on for the very first time? Probably wonderful. How did you feel when you were wearing a suit, if you've ever worn one? Most likely in first place. That is something that I have absolutely experienced.

One thing that contributes to your ability to feel well is increasing the likelihood that you will dress in a way that feels good to you. It's just one more thing that can help you feel fantastic about who you are and the choices you've made in life. It also helps people respond to you in a more favorable way, and when we receive results like making new friends or landing a new job, we feel better about ourselves as a result.

Consequently, devote part of your time to reevaluating and modernizing your existing outfit.

If you've seen most of my videos, you've probably noticed that I wear mostly black or blue shirts, but I try to choose clothes that are comfortable and make me feel good.

The verb

Take a glance at the clothes in your closet. Make a note of the clothes that you enjoy wearing and those that you prefer not to wear. Then, separate the items into two separate lists: "keep" and "get rid of."

In addition to this, whenever you go shopping, regardless of whether it is online or in person, give some thought to the kinds of clothes that would make you feel amazing when you wore them. Keep looking if the thing is just a maybe or if it won't make you feel amazing if you try it on. It is not necessary to spend a lot of money; all you need are a few deals on things that you know will make you feel good about yourself.

Having said that, I've just been browsing the sales at Abercrombie & Fitch on their website....

Jonny, pay attention to what you're writing throughout the rest of the book!

How To Quit Thinking In A Pessimistic Way

In the end, if you find that you are preoccupied with all of that pessimistic thinking, there is some encouraging news for you: you may learn to triumph over it. There is no justification for you to continue to cycle through negative thought patterns in that way. You don't have to keep forcing yourself to cope with those feelings over and over again; instead, you can focus on learning how to let them go and go on.

The most crucial component of this book is learning how to overcome negative thinking. To be able to think positively, you must first learn to eliminate negative thinking from your life. This is not always an easy task, but it is necessary if you wish to think positively. However, if you are prepared to put in the effort and you are knowledgeable about what you are doing, it is possible to accomplish your goal. All that is required of you is to get started and educate yourself on what it is that you are doing.

Within the context of this chapter, we are going to have a discussion about the fundamental idea of getting rid of negative ideas. If you can figure out how to prevail over them, you can rest assured that your long-term prospects are going to be far brighter. You are able to have the confidence that, in the end, you are going to be successful in your relationships with yourself, and you will be able to let go of all of that negativity.

Negativity builds up inside of us over time, and we cannot begin to truly move on in life unless we are able to release it in an appropriate manner. This is not always an easy task, but it is necessary in order to make progress. Having said that, doing so is a fairly straightforward process. As you go through this chapter, keep in mind some of the ways in which you can start to follow these steps and get started on your own journey to rid your life of negativity. You are making an effort to get rid of your negative ideas so that you may make room in your life for the positive ones that will come after them. This is quite important, and if you are unable to make it happen, you will most likely have a difficult time. You are going to have to make sure that you are putting in a lot of effort, and you are going to have to follow these instructions.

After going through the primary steps to overcoming negativity, we are going to take a minute to pause and think about the ways in which you may begin to seek the changes in your life that will lead to the changes that you are seeking for. In other words, we are going to consider the ways in which you can begin to seek the changes that will lead to the changes that you are looking for. You will be shown some of the most effective strategies that can be implemented in order to triumph over unfavorable circumstances. Even though you will only receive a brief summary at the outset of the book, it is essential that you keep in mind that, as you move forward through the material, you will be provided with additional details. Throughout the course of reading this book, you will have the opportunity to acquire the knowledge necessary to engage in cognitive restructuring, positivism, and a great deal more.

Let's get started right away, shall we? It is not necessary for there to be any fear involved in changing your thoughts. It is possible for you to accomplish this goal if you are ready to put in the necessary effort and labor. You are capable of accomplishing this. This is something you will do. You just need to have the desire to succeed and be willing to put in the effort. If you are able to commit yourself to thinking these positive thoughts, you will find that altering your mind is not nearly as difficult as you originally believed it would be.

Accept Responsibility For The Issue

You have to admit that there is a problem before you can do anything else. You cannot fix it if you refuse to admit that it is there, and with this step, you are going to be getting rid of it. This is true for just about anything that you want to fix, and it is important to keep this in mind. You want to make sure that, eventually, the methods in which you engage with those around you are going to be positive, and having that aim inevitably lends itself to admitting that, at that point in time, there is some negativity that needs to be relieved to succeed in what you're trying to accomplish. You need to be acknowledged, and you want to make sure that you can find a way to acquire the positive that you are seeking for.

Do You Want to Adapt?

One more precondition for being able to triumph over one's own negativity is the desire to alter one's behavior in the first place. It is necessary to have the desire to believe that you can change or that you can alter the way in which you engage with the world that surrounds you in order to be successful. Another challenging aspect is acknowledging that the issue you were facing was a genuine one and that things need to shift as quickly as possible in order to avoid further complications. You need to be able to figure out how to best work with yourself and within your own beliefs in order to make sure that you can reconcile with that idea and that stress of grappling with the fact that you spent so much of your life and your energy doing something that you are now trying to defeat as quickly and readily as you can. In order to do this, you need to be able to figure out how to best work with yourself and within your own beliefs.

Take Accountability for Your Actions

Making sure that you are able to take and accept responsibility is the third stage in assuring that you will be able to receive the change that you have been striving for with all of your heart. You have to take responsibility for your role in the process of what holds you back. You won't be able to start processing what has happened unless you are able to accept and acknowledge what was place as well as how you were participating in it. When you come to terms with the fact that you have both the power and the duty to effect the changes that are necessary, you will finally be in a position to do so. Some people will have a hard time with this, but you can make it work.

Try to Make Some Adjustments

At this time, all of the effort that has been put in up until now will finally pay off. You are at the point where you need to start proactively making those changes in order to improve your ability to begin working toward either the life you want to have or the thing that you want to have. It can take place in a great variety of different ways; nonetheless, there are a select handful that are much more typical than the rest. The following is a list of some of the most frequent ways that can be used to overcome negative thoughts:

Talking therapy

You can learn how to fix your cognitive processes by participating in therapy, which is something that can be obtained in a wide variety of different formats. When this happens, what you really need is someone who can guide you through the process of comprehending what has to be done as well as how you are feeling. Once you have this information, you can begin to figure out how to handle difficult situations in a more effective manner. This is also beneficial if you discover that you are not making progress on your own or if you get the sense that, ultimately, you need to figure out some manner in which you can better deal with the problems that are occurring around you. When you have a therapist on your team, they will be able to walk you through everything you will need to know in order to have a better understanding of the way in which you are going to approach a particular circumstance. Because they will be there for you and guide you through the process of coping, which is extremely strong and helpful, you will have a greater ability to respond to negative or stressful situations.

Maintaining Command Of The Most Vital Feelings

Over the course of the previous few years, the amount of time spent conducting research on feelings has steadily grown. Theories that attempt to identify what emotions are and where they come from have received important contributions from a diverse range of academic disciplines, including neuroscience, medicine, sociology, history, and computer science. The goal of the research that is now being carried out is to determine what exactly triggers these feelings and the role that they play for an individual.

Emotions can be either a pleasant or unpleasant experience, and they are frequently associated with a distinct pattern of physiological activity. They bring about some alterations in the functioning of an individual's behavior as well as their physiological systems. According to the Oxford Dictionary, it is a powerful emotion that arises as a consequence of an individual's circumstances, mood, and the nature of their interactions with other people. They are referred to as the reactions that we have in response to significant internal and external occurrences.

There are four different manifestations of emotions, which are occurrences, dispositions, fleeting states, and more permanent states.

Psychotherapists believe that feelings can be anywhere on a scale from mild to extreme. They have a series of responses that are typically coordinated with one another. The mechanisms behind the reactions can be categorized as either behavioral, verbal, physiological, or neurological. The term "emotion" can also be described as a person's strong feelings that they direct toward a particular subject or person. Emotions can also be used to refer to moderate events or thoughts that are not specifically directed to anything else. This is a different usage of the term, but it is still relevant.

Joseph LeDoux defines emotions in a way that is applicable to everyday life as the result of conscious and cognitive processes that consistently take place anytime the bodily system is reacting to a stimulus. On the other hand, psychologists and other mental health professionals define emotions as a more nuanced form of feeling that is accompanied by both bodily and psychological shifts that have an effect on an individual's thought process and behavior. The social sciences characterize feelings in terms of the significant functions that they play in the culture of human beings and the day-to-day interactions of those people.

Constituents of an Affective State

Scherer's component processing model of emotions was developed by Klaus Rainer Scherer, a previous expert in the field of psychology. This model defines the five important components of a passion and how they work together. For a sensation to be classified as an emotion, all of its constituent parts must function in concert with one another. When an emotional episode takes place, the following sequence of events takes place, and it describes how the various components are put together.

An individual's subjective assessment of a stimuli in their environment is known as their cognitive appraisal of that stimulus. It is a description of how an individual makes sense of an event, which in turn influences how an individual makes sense of a circumstance. It is the manner in which a person interprets and swiftly reacts to triggers that occur in everyday life. In general, it refers to the manner in which individuals judge the events and things that occur in their lives.

During an emotional experience, a person may experience a variety of bodily symptoms, which are the result of biological processes.

Habitual patterns of behavior: This component serves as a motivator by assisting in the process of developing and directing an individual's motor responses.

An emotional response is inextricably linked to the act of expressing oneself because expressiveness is an essential component of any feeling. They contribute to the communication of how an individual behaves as well as the actions that the individual intends to take.

When an emotional state takes place, a person will go through a series of unique experiences that we refer to as feelings.

Alterations That Occur During Feelings

When someone is feeling emotional, they will always experience changes in both their internal and exterior states.

Alterations in one's external appearance are those that can be observed when an emotion is being experienced. Changes in an individual's voice, facial expression, and body language, such as movement of the hands and legs, sweating, forehead creases, erection of hair on the head, or redness in the eyes, can all help to describe the type of emotion an individual is going through. Changes in an individual's facial expression, such as a wrinkled forehead, erected hair on the head, or redness in the eyes, can also help to describe the feeling.

Internal changes are occurrences that cannot be directly witnessed but always result from a particular stimulus. These kinds of changes take place in response to a stimulus. The ANS of a typical human being is bifurcated into two halves. When an individual is confronted with a potentially dangerous situation, their sympathetic ANS assists in preparing their bodies to respond appropriately. In this scenario, a person will prepare himself to either engage in combat or flee the situation. The parasympathetic branch of the autonomic nervous system (ANS) helps restore the energy that an individual expends either in the process of avoiding or of dealing with a particular occurrence. Some of the changes that take place on the inside of a person during an emotion are an increase in the rate of heartbeats, an increase in the levels of blood sugar, rapid respiration, an alteration in the frequency of brain waves, dilation of the pupils, a decrease in the secretion of saliva that results in a dry mouth, and decreased functioning of the gastrointestinal tract. As a result, an individual will not feel hungry while they are experiencing an emotion.

How To Improve Your Own Self-Confidence

Affirmations are a helpful tool for boosting one's self-confidence. You need to place yourself in a scenario in which you are content with what you are doing and you need to achieve this as soon as possible. Consider the activities that you are certain to take pleasure in, and check to see that the proportion of those activities that contribute to your sense of fulfillment is more than that of the pursuits that lead to your uncertainty.

For instance, composing poetry was one of my favorite things to do. Even if it wasn't going to help me make a living, it was something I was really good at doing. I kept a journal, and within that journal, I would place copies of my poems that I had written. That was a workout I did in the morning. Since I enjoyed listening to music, I decided to teach myself how to play an instrument. Because of this, I now have a great deal of self-assurance because when you play the piano, you tend to assume that you are performing in a concert setting. When I play my guitar, I put every feeling I have into it, and I am confident that my playing is getting better despite the fact that the music may not be played perfectly. These are uplifting and delightful experiences that contribute to my increased self-confidence. I used to claim "I cannot do the F chord" on the guitar, yet all it took was practice for me to finally be able to play it. The more you engage in activities that you take pleasure in, the more proficient you will become in them.

Although I have never used affirmations, I think you could say that I make positive statements, which some people would interpret as using affirmations. When I have a goal that I want to accomplish, rather than telling myself that it would be difficult or giving up before I even begin, I remind myself, "I can do this." When other people look at themselves in the mirror, they repeat this to themselves like a mantra because they find that it gives them the strength to accomplish their goals. Follow the path that yields the best results for you, since you can be sure that something will. If you keep looking for activities that you take pleasure in doing, you will soon be able to organize the entirety of your life around those pursuits. To give you an example, I was quite good at reading. My passion for reading led me to discover that I might use this talent to read aloud to children at the local library. It assisted me in breaking out of my comfort zone and allowed me to spend time doing something that I valued and was confident in my ability to achieve.

But I forced myself to keep trying, and eventually I was able to read books that were hundreds of pages long. If there are activities in your life that are challenging to accomplish, try switching the times that you do those things. The early, when you have more energy, is the best time to focus on challenging projects. The optimum environment for intense reading is a quiet one. It's possible that you're not realizing your full potential because you're allowing life to get in the way of your goals. In addition, meditation was useful because it encouraged me to shift my emphasis away from unhelpful ways of thinking and toward achieving positive outcomes in my life. I found that I was able to derive an increasing amount of satisfaction from participating in activities that I enjoyed despite the fact that my life was otherwise very hectic. If you can find a job that you enjoy doing, it is best to take it, even if the income is lower, since the dividend that you get is that you are less worried and feel so much better capable of handling whatever comes your way. This is the perfect situation. Because my job suits both my personality and my temperament, I am quite good at it. This helps me achieve a high level of success. The job is tailor-made for me in every way.

You need to take a look at your fundamental beliefs. Be familiar with their nature. The majority of persons who struggle with low self-esteem tend to have more positive thoughts about other people than they do about themselves. The helping professions provide an excellent setting for uncovering hidden aspects of oneself. They also assist you in gaining perspective on the situation at hand. Help yourself feel better about who you are by donating part of your time to organizations that serve the homeless or by assisting friends who have families. The feeling of accomplishment that comes from accomplishing goals like these gives life a sense of purpose, and in the process, you start to realize that you are valuable and that you are gaining confidence. It is important to keep in mind that you can improve both your experience and your sense of self-worth by practicing mindfulness while participating in the activities described below and by keeping a happy attitude as much as possible.

You have troubles with self-esteem because you allow yourself to be influenced by what other people say or think about you, and this is the main reason for it. Write down every unfavorable event or circumstance in your life that causes you to feel dread, and then immediately refute those events or circumstances. Do not allow yourself to be defined by what the opinions of other people are.

Make the most of your setbacks by viewing them as stepping stones to greater achievement. Don't be scared to accept that you went about something in the wrong way; instead, use the lessons you've learned and try doing things in a different method that turns out to be more successful. It is all about expanding your talents, and as you do so, you will grow more confident in yourself and be more in charge of any given scenario. The key is to focus on getting better at what you do.

Overcoming Adverse Experiences

Injury comes when we are looked with any dreadful circumstance, such as a car accident, fire, witness to a mishap, catastrophic event, an assault on your person, war, and so on. There are many different thoughts and feelings that are associated with a traumatic experience. When people are trying to recover from a traumatic incident, there are a lot of people who will rationally block out the experience that caused them so much suffering, while other people will remember it constantly. A person may experience a range of emotions after suffering an injury, including:

- Disbelief — Disbelief is a typical reaction to any traumatic experience, and the more directly you were involved in the experience, the more disbelief will set in. Your brain needs time to analyze the horrific images you've witnessed, and this is the point at which feelings of shock begin to set in. The feelings of shock will take some time to process since your mind requires time to do so.

- A strong feeling that what one has witnessed just could not have taken place in any way, shape, or form. This is a common reaction among people who are confronted with a situation that is shocking to them.

- Denial, in which multiple persons refuse to acknowledge that the event took place and instead strive to make it sound implausible.

- Emotional suffering – even if you were physically unharmed in the event, you will still sense the emotional suffering of those who were hurt because you will be surrounded by them.

- Anger: Following the shaking caused by the earthquake, you may feel enraged and question yourself, "Why has this happened to me?" You may also feel enraged toward anybody and everyone.

• Accusing ourselves or others for what has happened is something that we do all the time. Sometimes we even criticize God for allowing anything bad to happen in our lives.

• Melancholy — After successfully completing a particularly harrowing meeting, you may find that you are suddenly overcome with waves of melancholy emotion.

• Depression – for a considerable amount of time after the event, you can all of a sudden fall into a state of melancholy now and then. • Anxiety – uneasiness frequently results from fear, and it can continue for a considerable amount of time after the experience.

The bulk of the aforementioned feelings and concerns are among the most commonly recognized ones that are associated with having undergone an injury; these feelings can arise without any explicit request and at any time. What you need to realize is that these feelings are normal and are your body and brain's way of adapting to what has happened. Both the feelings and the contemplations will eventually go away with the passage of time. This is something that you should be aware of. There are many methods in which you can adjust to them and take control of them, but the path that is best suited to you will clearly be determined by the severity of the injury to which you were exposed. There are many ways in which you can adapt to them and take control of them. However, there are a variety of different adaptive skills that may be learned in order to assist you in protecting yourself against injury.

• Changing your condition • Taking part in recreational activities • Picking up your regular day-to-day schedule • Participating in workshops • Accepting what happened and moving on with life • Taking about what occurred and allowing it to become permanent • Listening to and tolerating advice from family, friends, or a professional advisor • Accepting what happened and moving on with life • Accepting what happened and moving on with life • Taking about what occurred and allowing it to become permanent • Taking about what occurred and allowing

People Who Are More Introverted And Their Relationships

The Obstacles You Face and Some Useful Advice to Improve Your Relationships (With Friends and Your Partner, for Men and Women)

Because of this circumstance, the introvert may find that they are required to step outside of their comfort zones in order to continue cultivating the relationships that they have developed and that they treasure.

The thing about introverts is that, for the most part, they will typically build relationships that they want to establish. This is something that sets them apart from extroverts. People who an introvert chooses to associate with, or those with whom they choose to spend time, are typically people that the introvert enjoys having nearby.

As an introvert, you are going to run into troubles in relationships from time to time, just like anyone else who is in a relationship. In spite of this, though, things are made somewhat more difficult by the fact that you are an introvert. Take, for instance:

Variations in the Methods of Communication

How often have you and the other individuals in your life gotten into arguments? If we are completely candid, the answer is yes, a couple of times, provided that the relationship is strong.

Now, when you look at things from your point of view, you frequently take the time right after a little of conflict to momentarily get lost in your thoughts. This is because you believe that your viewpoint is the most accurate. Because of this, the person in your life might start to interpret this as a sign that you are trying to steer clear of them, when in fact, you are just allowing yourself the time to sort out your ideas, as you are wont to do in situations like these.

People who are extroverts typically find that they are better able to respond when the situation is fast-paced. In the event that you are an introvert and you start dating an extrovert, the disparity in the ways in which the two of you communicate may result in some conflict between the two of you.

Communication is essential to the maintenance of a happy and fulfilling relationship. Therefore, as an introvert, you have a tendency to place little value and emphasis on the real-world relationships that you have. This can lead to a nasty breakdown in communication, which is only the first step in a gradual decrease in the connection's value.

As was mentioned, some introverts also suffer from shyness, which means that they will have an even more difficult time speaking effectively owing to their lack of confidence and their fear while interacting with others in social situations. This circumstance has the potential to destroy the relationship.

In a Conflict, One's Silence May Be Misunderstood as Aggression.

How many different instances of violent confrontation have you been a part of? I'm guessing more than a couple times, is that correct?

The problem is that introverts, with their reserved manner and tendency toward calmness, do not often show the whole range of feelings that they experience. When they are angry, they will often talk with composure, and when things do reach to a head, rather than burst (unless they are severely pushed), an introvert will sit back silently and contemplate. When they are angry, they will often talk with composure. Have you completed the task already?

Now, a good many of the individuals out here are extroverted. They are aware that conflict is a form of interaction that involves both parties making attacks on one another. On the other hand, in this situation, the fact that you are remaining cool and silent may be interpreted as a lack of concern or as evidence that you do not appreciate what the other person is saying. When your manager confronts you at work, you can inexplicably send the message that you do not take seriously what they are saying, especially if the confrontation takes place while you are at work.

though you have a disagreement with your significant other, you run the risk of coming across as arrogant and indifferent, even though neither of these things are actually true about you. If you do not take appropriate precautions, this circumstance may result in a breakdown in communication, which may have a negative impact on your relationships, which are very important to you.

Needs That Don't Align With Those of Your Partner or Friends

When you date someone who is more extroverted than you are, there is a greater potential that your personalities may overlap and become acquainted with one another.

You have become accustomed to spending the most of your free time by yourself, perhaps cuddled up on the couch with a good book or watching a movie. Here you are. After that, you find yourself in a relationship, and all of a sudden, you have to organize time to hang out with your new significant other.

Even while these kinds of issues can be worked out via conversation, there is still frequently that feeling of dissatisfaction when you push yourself to get out more and become more outgoing, which might result in regular disagreements between you and your spouse.

If you go out with your partner and they want to take a picture of you, you are going to have to oblige them even if the thought of doing so makes you feel awkward. These kinds of predicaments come up all the time and frequently result in confrontations.

You don't enjoy talking about yourself too much, do you?

Imagine that you are going on a date for the first time. Wow! butterflies and anything else! When you finally get there, though, you get the sudden realization that you might not be all that interested in talking about yourself to this new individual. It's possible that after a few dates, you won't feel completely at ease.

The desire of many introverts to keep certain aspects of themselves private usually comes at the expense of their ability to form meaningful relationships.

To have meaningful relationships with other people, we need to get comfortable with the idea of exposing our weaknesses to them. This helps to cultivate trust among people and allows for deeper bonds to be formed between them.

Even though an introvert will jump at the chance to forge meaningful connections with other people, they will typically do so in the vain hope that they would be able to keep others from learning too much about themselves in the process. In most cases, it is not due to the fact that they have something to conceal. It's possible that they were feeling overwhelmed at the time, or that they weren't quite as invested in the relationship as they are now. Introverts tend to take their time getting to know people, which can make it difficult for their extroverted friends and partners to form meaningful connections with them.

Because you don't want to talk about yourself, you can come off as uninterested, and your partner might take this as an indication that you don't appreciate them. If you don't want to talk about yourself, then don't talk about yourself.

Thinking too much

Hey, it's awesome to be able to think! You undoubtedly are aware of that. However, as is the case with everything else, doing too much of it might lead to complications.

Because introverts have a natural inclination to become concerned with details, planning, observing, and deciphering, it is common for them to approach practically everything from the viewpoint of a thinker.

When you go shopping, you tend to become fixated on the options that are available to you. The jam has too much sugar in it, but you are out of the marmalade you wanted to use. The alternate jelly appears to be tasty; but, it is manufactured by a brand that you are unfamiliar with; the third choice, on the other hand, shows promise. The fourth alternative seems to be a shoddy imitation of the one you like best. The fifth choice is rather far down on the list, and so on.

The folks that are a part of your life might find this problem to be quite bothersome. Your fixation on particulars, which stems from your strong desire to reach the best possible conclusion, may drive a gulf between you and the people in your immediate environment.

If this happens, it's possible that your close friends and romantic partners would shun you because they see you to be becoming monotonous.

Overthinking anything might make you appear shallow and conceited, but in the long run, it can be detrimental to your success since it causes you to become trapped in the dilemma of choice, and as a result, you can select the alternative that is less desirable.

You Have Difficulty Working in a Team Environment

As has been mentioned previously, introverts find enormous comfort in the company of alone themselves. When you are by alone, which is probably the most of the time, you come up with new ideas, write stories, and make artwork. You play around with different ideas, thoughts, and notions in your head. In essence, you transform into your own personal library.

However, when you go out with your pals, you suddenly find that you are a part of a larger group. All of a sudden, doors that have been open in your thoughts begin to shutter. The tales that you had planned to share are confined within you. Because of the large number of individuals in the area, engaging in conversation depletes all of your energy. You become quiet in the group because you are unable to access the thoughts that are running through your head, and this gives the impression that you are merely a hanger-on. Even when you try to convince your friends that you cherish the relationship that you have with them, they start to believe that you do not value it. It appears that your behaviors do not reflect what you say.

Being an introvert makes it challenging to thrive in environments that value extroversion as a dominant personality trait.

Because of this, there may be tension between you and the people you consider to be your friends. You will give the impression that you are arrogant and unwilling to participate in the conversations, when the reality is that you are not really able to access your best thoughts when you are in the company of other people. As an introvert, you probably find this quite frustrating as well. You are unable to fully describe why you are unable to think clearly while you are in the company of other people. As a consequence of this, it is challenging to establish a relationship with other people.

If it gets to the point in your romantic relationship that your spouse begins to see that you love being alone, possibly even more than you enjoy being with them, they will begin to remove themselves from you because they will realize that you do not require their presence in your life.

1.2 Regard for Oneself

When delving into this topic, it is important that you conduct some self-reflection. There are certain individuals who are aware that they possess a particular amount of self-esteem. There are some people who will have severe issues with their self-esteem, but they will not be aware that they have these issues until one day, by some stroke of luck, they find it out. Numerous studies have been conducted on the topic of anxiety in relation to self-esteem. To begin, let's discuss Erikson's stages of development and how they connect to one's sense of self-worth.

Because people will always be going through one of Erikson's phases of development no matter where in life they are, using Erikson's stages as a framework for discussing self-esteem is an excellent way to frame the problem. Therefore, by taking a look at the many stages that are outlined in this model, we can get a better idea of where the tension might be coming from in a person's condition. It is possible that whatever is causing the issue with one's self-esteem is connected to the topic that Erikson identifies as being essential to successfully traverse each stage.

From birth to death, according to Erikson's theory, there are eight stages of development that occur in humans. In order to finish and integrate the process, the steps need to be moved. The transition from one stage to the next may look very different for different people. The age at which development begins will vary substantially from one individual to the next.

The first step that Erikson outlined is the battle between "trust" and "mistrust." Erikson felt that throughout this stage, which lasts from birth to eighteen months, a child is developing trust for the primary caregiver, who is most often the mother. This is the first impulse that humans are born with. At this point, the unborn child understands that it will not remain in the mother's womb for the rest of its life and that it will eventually become an independent being. On the other hand, the infant is defenseless and must quickly learn to place their faith in whoever is caring for them because they cannot protect themselves. This is a significant psychic shock, one that the majority of people do not have a good grasp on, and that is what creates the tension for Erikson during this first stage of his development.

The second stage lasts between one and three years and is characterized by the conflict between the concepts of "autonomy" and "shame." This stage occurs between the ages of one and three years. During this stage, a kid is learning that they can walk around the room and walk away from their parents. During this stage, a child is able to walk around the room. They will begin to interact with the world as an autonomous creature and will begin to become aware of their bodily space as well as the manner in which they navigate the world around them. Willpower is the attribute that needs to be cultivated in this environment. Will is what drives us forward in this world and keeps us moving forward.

The third stage is a battle between "initiative" and "guilt." This typically takes place between the ages of three and five. When children reach this age, they begin to develop the capacity to interact with the world around them, and they may also begin to engage in social interactions with other children. It takes "initiative" to begin anything new and see it through to completion. The feeling known as "guilt" occurs when a person believes they have behaved inappropriately. Children frequently get these tendencies confused and end up feeling guilty for the behavior they are attempting to initiate. If the youngster is unable to properly process both their triumphs and mistakes, they can be overcome with a sense of guilt, and as a result, they might be unable to go on to the next stage. The most important quality to possess in this situation is "purpose." A youngster who is in this period of development needs to cultivate a sense of self that has established that he or she is deserving of initiative rather than guilt.

The following step compares "industry" with "inferiority." This is a significant and crucial stage that lasts for around seven years and is occupied by youngsters aged five to twelve years old. It takes approximately seven years to master this stage. When a youngster is taught to perform something that they enjoy and are skilled at, we say that "industry" has become steady. Around the start of this period, children are expected to begin meeting the requirements set forth by institutions and other organizations such as schools. They are going to be required to learn behaviors and become proficient in them. These begin with relatively straightforward activities and progressively become more complicated. The ways in which a youngster learns to deal with adversity will become defining characteristics of their maturation as a person. They will acquire a sense of industry if they are taught to accept some level of failure and rejection and if they continue to work despite these setbacks. This works extremely well if a youngster learns something that they are naturally talented at and also enjoy doing, such as a sport or an art form. Competence is the most important quality in this regard. In order for a youngster to advance to the next stage, they will need to learn how to develop a sense of competence.

The fifth stage is called "identity" versus "role confusion," and it occurs between the ages of twelve and eight. This conflict takes place. When a child reaches this age, they come to terms with their attraction to other people and begin to form friendships that have the potential to mature into positive partnerships. Children and adolescents who are in this stage will learn how to have friends and how to be good team players. "Fidelity" is the primary attribute that characterizes this period. At this point in their development, children are taught the fundamentals of adulthood. For example, they discover how to pay attention while sitting in a classroom setting and how to identify activities and interests that appeal to them. They are given more leeway to behave as they like, and they are given the respect due to actual adults. If a person is not progressing through this stage well, it may indicate that they lack the self-esteem to develop aspects of their life that are underdeveloped, which will lead to a pattern of unease that could increase their suffering. If this is the case, the individual may be suffering from low self-esteem.

The years between the ages of eighteen and forty are characterized by the quest to discover a love relationship that is significant to oneself, and Erikson refers to this period as "intimacy" as opposed to "isolation." At this point, a person is required to become fully integrated into society and to establish a family structure of some kind, irrespective of the size of that system. It may take a long time for people to get to this stage, but there is a natural need within humans to form romantic relationships with other people, and it is during this period that someone will do so. Now, this does not imply that this school of psychology mandates that people must be in monogamous, conventional relationships; rather the contrary, in fact. This indicates that everyone has a natural desire to be in a loving relationship, preferably one that is secure and fulfilling, as well as one that allows them to advance rather than retreat in their own development. At this point, love should be the focus of your attention.

After this stage, you will either experience "creativity" or "stagnation." This spans the years between the ages of forty and sixty-five, and it is at this time that an individual has the opportunity to leave behind some sort of enduring legacy in the latter portion of their life. It is possible that it will be through children and grandkids, but it is also possible that it will not be. It may come from a very enduring piece of art, or it could come from a truly enduring relationship. Someone might be a philanthropist, and they might consider this to be their contribution to the world that will live on after they are gone. This, along with the primary virtue of care, is something that needs to be developed during this stage.

Erikson contends that after the age of sixty-five, "wisdom" is the most important virtue to cultivate, and that the most challenging situations that everyone must go through are those that include ego, integrity, and despair. When a person reaches this age, they are required to reflect on their life and come to grips with what they have accomplished; it may be difficult for some individuals to think about their lives in these terms. Others will pass away in a tranquil manner.

At each of these stages, there is a fundamental tension that, if it is not resolved, would result in a significant decrease in the individual's sense of self-worth. Whenever someone is having issues with their self-esteem, it may be traced back to one of the fundamental problems that Erikson describes. These are some fundamental realities that must be confronted by each one of us.

Boosting One's Self-Confidence Is Beneficial To Both One's Physical And Mental Health.

The professionals who work at the National Mental Health Centre believe that having a healthy self-esteem and sufficient self-confidence are the primary indicators of excellent mental wellbeing. As we have previously discovered in an earlier section of this book, the formation of a person's sense of self-worth typically takes place in the formative years of childhood, when the individual's parents are largely responsible for shaping both their self-assurance and their personality. Children who were raised in households that were more upbeat and encouraging tend to carry more confidence with them throughout their lives. This gives them an advantage in a variety of spheres, including academics, athletics, social skills, and even just taking better care of themselves in general. When youngsters reach their teenage years, those who have developed a healthy sense of self-confidence are more equipped to deal with the influence of their peers and are able to make choices that are in their own long-term interests.

According to the mind-body connection theory, a person's mental health can have an impact on their physical health, and similarly, a person's physical health can have an impact on their mental health. People who struggle with mental illnesses such as depression and anxiety frequently experience deterioration in their physical health, manifesting itself in symptoms such as persistent pain or a lowered resistance to illness. It is possible for a person to enhance their physical health by taking care of oneself physically, such as by engaging in physical activity and maintaining a nutritious diet. However, maintaining a healthy mental state can also assist a person avoid developing physical issues.

Because they are able to participate in a wider variety of activities, people who enjoy better physical health typically report higher levels of happiness and life satisfaction. They often have more energy and motivation to get themselves out into the world in order to accomplish things, or even just to connect with other people. People have a natural tendency to derive pleasure from the good fortune of others; hence, when they surround themselves with people who exude self-assurance and contentment, they may also start to experience these emotions themselves. People who are confident tend to hang out in the same social circles for this reason, which is why you frequently see them doing so. People who have strong mental health are drawn to others who have the same qualities and would much rather spend their time with such people than with those who do not display the same characteristics.

How To Commit To A New Year's Resolution

People frequently say things like, "I am aware that this is significant to me, but I am just not that motivated." These individuals rarely begin anything new or make any changes because they wait to be motivated before they do so. They seem to believe, for some reason, that the only way they can move closer to anything (or further away from something) is if they are motivated. Not true!

They somehow have the expectation that inspiration will materialize out of thin air, and that this will enchant them into taking action in the direction of their goal. Do not sit around hoping for motivation to somehow materialize on its own because it does not, and it will not. No matter how long you wait, the motivation bus will never come. You might as well give up.

What comes next is a statement of the utmost significance.

DO NOT wait until you feel motivated or until you get motivated.

If what you want to do is essential to you but you don't feel motivated to work toward it, you should force yourself to complete the task regardless of how you feel about it. Make the conscious choice to carry it out. It is possible that an act of will, discipline, and determination will be required to accomplish this. Yes, it is possible that it will be unpleasant, that it will need a commitment from you, and that you may be required to forego doing something else.

Nevertheless, you carry it out because you are aware of the final result, which is your objective; this is more important than whether or not you are feeling motivated at the time. The majority of people make the mistake of concentrating on what they will be required to sacrifice rather than what they will stand to gain in the long run.

Do you seriously believe that elite swimmers look forward to getting up at 4:30 in the morning on a daily basis to train? They are totally focused on the end result; their objective, rather than resenting the fact that they have to get up early in the morning. That is what propels them forward, and it is what serves as their primary source of inspiration.

What is it that you value the most?

Just get things going in the right direction in order to make progress toward a goal that is significant to you. Begin to push that ball of motivation until it gains its own momentum, which it will, and once it does, it might even be difficult to top. As the well-known slogan for Nike proclaims, 'Just Do It!' Or, to paraphrase a well-known quote often attributed to Johann Wolfgang von Goethe: "Whatever you can do or dream you can, begin it." The phrase "boldness has genius, power, and magic in it"

It's similar to starting an exercise routine for the first time after a long hiatus or possibly never before. It is exceedingly unlikely that you will roll out of bed one morning brimming with inspiration and eager to get started working out.

You might not feel like it, but you know that if you do it, in the long run it will make you feel better and keep you healthier, so you force yourself to get moving even though you don't want to. At first, it will require a significant amount of effort, and you may find that you have to struggle against the little voice in your head that will present you with a variety of compelling reasons and opportunities to avoid doing it.

This is a really significant point. The more you engage in the activity, the more inspired you will feel! The more that pressure is applied to the ball, the more momentum will be created by the ball itself. It's the same as trying to push a rock up a hill. When you push a rock up one side of a hill, it becomes progressively more difficult to do so as you approach the crest of the hill.

The moment that most people should be making their breakthrough is the one in which they throw in the towel. However, if you push that rock over the edge, it will generate its own momentum, causing it to roll downhill more quickly and for a longer distance as it continues to build up more momentum.

So keep that in mind. It's not always going to be easy to find the motivation to work on the things that are most important to you. Don't sit around and wait for the motivation to strike you. Make the decision to carry it out anyway, and then get started building momentum. You will soon discover that the momentum will continue even without your participation, and it is possible that it may even pull you along with it.

www.ingramcontent.com/pod-product-compliance
Lightning Source LLC
Chambersburg PA
CBHW050247120526
44590CB00016B/2246